World's Best Rugby Jokes

in this series:

The World's Best Acting Jokes
The World's Best After-Dinner Jokes
The World's Best Boss Jokes
The World's Best Business Jokes
The World's Best Cricket Jokes
The World's Best Dirty Jokes
More of the World's Best Dirty Jokes
Still More of the World's Best Dirty Jokes
The World's Best Dirty Limericks
The World's Best Dirty Songs
The World's Best Dirty Stories
The World's Best Doctor Jokes
The World's Best Drinking Jokes
The World's Best Fishing Jokes
The World's Best Football Jokes
The World's Best Golf Jokes
More of the World's Best Golf Jokes
The World's Best Holiday Jokes
The World's Best Irish Jokes
Still More of the World's Best Irish Jokes
The World's Best Jewish Jokes
More of the World's Best Jewish Jokes
The World's Best Lawyer Jokes
The World's Best Lightbulb Jokes
The World's Best Marriage Jokes
The World's Best Men Jokes
The World's Best Motoring Jokes
The World's Best Sailing Jokes
The World's Best Scottish Jokes
The World's Best Skiing Jokes
The World's Best Women Jokes

The World's Best Rugby Jokes

Edward Phillips

ILLUSTRATED BY
ANDY HUNT

HarperCollins*Publishers*

HarperCollins*Publishers*
77–85 Fulham Palace Road,
Hammersmith, London W6 8JB

A Paperback Original 1997
1 3 5 7 9 8 6 4 2

A catalogue record for this book
is available from the British Library

ISBN 0 00 638866 3

Photoset in Linotron Goudy Old Style by
Rowland Phototypesetting Limited
Bury St Edmunds, Suffolk

Printed and bound in Great Britain by
Caledonian International Book Manufacturing Limited,
Glasgow

The scrum-half had just suffered a severe blow in the region of his essential equipment. The trainer ran onto the field with his first-aid gear and as he approached the injured player who was squirming on the ground with his hands clutched between his legs, the scrum-half moaned, 'Please, don't rub 'em! Just count 'em!'

'We'd like a suite, please,' said the newly-married English international to the receptionist at the London Hilton.

The receptionist looked at him and his lovely bride, and smiled. 'You'll be wanting the bridal, I suppose?' she said.

'Oh, no,' said the bride, blushing. 'I'll just hang on to his ears till I get used to it.'

'Why is it,' said the weedy little scrum-half to his attractive wife, 'that you never tell me when you have an orgasm?'

'Because, darling,' she replied, 'you're never there!'

Rugby Club Riddle

What is a 68?

You go down on me and I'll owe you one.

The wife of a rugby player, who was on extremely friendly terms with the rest of her husband's team, had to have an operation on her lower regions. When she got out of hospital, she went back to see the surgeon for a routine check.

'I'm afraid I have some bad news for you,' he said. 'By mistake, I left a small pair of surgical scissors inside you when I sewed you up!'

'Well, you'll have to get them out at once,' she said.

'Are they causing you any pain or discomfort?' asked the surgeon.

'No,' she replied, 'but two of my friends have cut their fingers, and one of them has been circumcised.'

Rugby Club Riddle

Which part of Popeye never gets rusty?
The part he keeps in Olive Oyl.

The rugby team celebrated their victory in the finals with a night on the town. One of the front row forwards ended up with a lady of the streets in her flat. After the act of sexual congress, he said, 'I'm sorry, love – if I'd known you were a virgin, I'd have been more gentle.'

'Virgin?' she said. 'You must be joking! If I'd have known you were going to be gentle, I'd 'ave taken me tights off!'

Two young kids were arguing in the street.

'My father is a better rugby player than your father!' said one.

'Maybe so,' said the other. 'But my mother's better than your mother!'

The first lad said, 'You may be right there. My Dad says the same thing.'

The full-back was big but not too bright, and the team was always ribbing him about his sex life.

'Is it true, Jacko,' he was asked in the changing rooms one day, 'that you've been trying out lots of new sexual positions?'

'Yeah,' said the big guy enthusiastically. 'I'm getting good, too! The next thing is to try them out with girls!'

Rugby Club Philosophy

If sex is simply a form of communication, can masturbation be described as 'talking to yourself'?

A couple of hulking front-row forwards were complaining to each other about the newfangled ideas being drilled into them by the club's new coach.

'It was so much simpler in the old days,' said one. 'You only had to remember one thing – kick ahead.'

'Yeah,' agreed his mate. 'Any head!'

A stunning young beauty walking down Piccadilly in a pair of skintight jeans caught the eye of a visiting rugger man from the Midlands who had come down to London for a big match.

'Excuse me, miss,' he said. 'I couldn't help wondering how on earth anyone could get into those jeans.'

'Well,' she replied, 'you could start by buying me a vodka Martini.'

'How are you feeling?' the team captain enquired sympathetically just before the big match.

'Not too good, Skipper,' said the scrum-half. 'I've still got this awful sore throat – can't seem to get rid of it.'

'I had the same problem a few weeks ago,' said the captain. 'Know how I got rid of it? Don't laugh – it really worked. I just got my wife to give me a blow-job – and it cleared up in no time! Why don't you try the same thing?'

'I'll do that!' said the scrum-half. 'Do you think your wife will be at home this evening?'

'Never mind that big second-row forward,' said the team captain to the diminutive fly-half just before the big match. 'Remember – the bigger they are, the harder they fall.'

'Yes, I know that,' said the fly-half. 'But what if he falls on *me*?'

TIMMBERRR!

Rugby Club Philosophy

Make love during the safe period – when her husband is playing in an away match.

Rugby-mad husband to long-suffering wife: 'No, my dear – *you* must decide. After all, it's *your* birthday, not mine. Shall we go and see the England–Scotland international, or the Blackheath–Harlequins game?'

A front-row forward visiting London for an important match at Twickenham got into a taxi in the West End and said to the cabbie, 'Where can I find the smallest and cheapest knocking-shop in London?'

The taxi-driver looked round and said, 'You're in it, mate!'

Overhead in the Changing Rooms

Full-back: 'Have you heard about these new washable condoms?'

Scrum-half: 'Yeah, I've tried them. They're OK – thinner and more sensitive. And they can be washed again and again. Mind you, I did get a nasty note from the laundry!'

The rugby full-back's wife was ironing her bra.

'I don't know why you bother,' he said. 'You've got nothing to put in it!'

'Well,' she said, 'I iron your underpants, don't I?'

The old groundsman was getting sick and tired of the young full-back's constant boasting about his sexual conquests. When they met in the local for a drink, he said, 'Listen – I'm sixty-seven and I make love nearly every night of the week.'

'Get away!' said the youngster disbelievingly.

'It's true,' said the old codger. 'I nearly made it on Monday, I nearly made it on Tuesday, I nearly made it on Wednesday . . .'

The referee took his girl to the cinema and while they were fooling around in the back row, his wig fell off. In groping around for it, his hand slid up his girlfriend's skirt.

'Yes!' she gasped. 'That's it! That's it!'

'It can't be,' said the ref. 'I part mine on the left.'

Rugby Club Philosophy

Sex is like a bank account. As soon as you withdraw, you lose interest.

He was known as one of the hardest and dirtiest tacklers in the game, but one afternoon he met his match, and the club secretary telephoned his wife with the news that he was coming home with a broken leg.

'Whose is it?' she enquired.

I used to play rugby professionally. In fact, I made quite a name for myself. I remember the day I returned from a match in Ireland. When I got off the plane at Heathrow, there was a crowd of several hundred, cheering and applauding. If you don't believe me, ask Will Carling. He was standing right beside me.

Freddie the Full-back: 'Hi there, gorgeous! Would you like to have sex?'
Young lady: 'Certainly not!'
Freddie the Full-back: 'Well, would you mind lying down while I do?'

First spectator: 'What do you think of our new stand-off half?'
Second spectator: 'Rubbish! I've had loose change move around in my pocket faster than him!'

AMBULANC

In my younger days, I used to play rugby professionally. Then my eyes went bad and I became a referee.

Overhead in the Changing Rooms

It was Ladies' Night at the rugby club. A woman walked into the ladies' room and was shocked to see a man using the toilet.

'Excuse me!' she said indignantly. 'This is for women only!'

'So's this!' he replied.

Rugby Club Riddle

What do you get when you cross a piranha with a prostitute?

Your last blow-job.

Did you hear about the front-row forward who read in a medical textbook that there were over 200 sexual positions, and asked the team captain where he could apply for one of them?

Scrum-half: 'You know those serial numbers they have on condoms?'
Full-back: 'I've never seen a serial number on a condom.'
Scrum-half: 'Oh? Maybe you've never rolled it back that far.'

First girl: 'Soccer players are terrific! They walk right up to you and put it straight in!'

Second girl: 'Rugby players are better! They put it in and then walk right up to you!'

Her ladyship picked up a hulking big rugby full-back in a bar and took him home for the night because she had been led to believe that men with big feet had big cocks.

The next morning, the rugger man woke up to find himself alone in the bed, with a £50 note pinned to the pillow, and a piece of paper with a message which read: 'Buy yourself a pair of shoes that fit!'

Two Division One players were discussing their wives in the bar one evening.

'My wife's as deaf as a post,' said one. 'I have to demonstrate everything to her to make her understand. When we played Featherstone Rovers, I had to wave a feather under her nose before she got it. And last week, when we played Saltburn, I had to wave the salt-cellar about before she understood.'

'You'll have a hell of a job next week, then,' said his mate. 'We're playing Cockermouth!'

Did you hear about the famous British Lions player who entered his dogs at Crufts? He got six months.

Rugby Club Riddle

What's a 72?

A 69 with three people watching.

Did you hear about the stand-off half who had a date with his girlfriend? She told him to bring some protection so he turned up at her apartment with two policemen.

The wife of the team captain was chatting to the wife of the club chairman over coffee one morning.

'My husband came home with a dozen roses last night,' she complained. 'That means I'm going to have to spend the whole weekend with my legs in the air!'

'Why?' asked her friend. 'Don't you have a vase?'

A rugby club manager was walking along the street one day carrying a camcorder. He met the manager of a rival club who asked him what it was for.

'I got it for Terry Jones,' was the reply. 'Our new wing-three-quarter.'

The other manager smiled and said, 'Sounds like a damned good swap to me!'

Rugby Club Philosophy

If masturbation stunts your growth, why do they always keep the dirty magazines on the top shelf?

A front-row forward was driving to Liverpool for an important match. On the way, he picked up a girl hitch-hiker, and halfway there, he put his hand on her knee.

'You can go further if you want,' she said softly. So he went on to Aberdeen.

The team captain of the Oldcastle Methodist Rugby Football Club was visiting London for a match. Walking along Piccadilly, he was shocked to see a young girl, about sixteen years old, lounging on a street corner, wearing a very short mini-skirt, a skimpy T-shirt, fishnet stockings, and high heels. He walked up to her and said,

'Young lady, what would your mother say if she saw you here like this?'

'She'd be furious,' said the girl. 'I'm on her corner!'

Rugby Club Riddle

What did one lesbian say to the other?

Your face or mine?

First rugby player: 'My wife is so frigid, she comes to bed with an ice cube in each hand and in the morning they haven't even begun to melt.'

Second rugby player: 'Well, my wife likes to have a glass of water by the side of her bed, and by the time she's carried it up from the kitchen, it's frozen solid.'

Third rugby player: 'That's nothing. My wife is so frigid, when she spreads her legs in bed at night, the central heating kicks on!'

'Sorry for missing that penalty kick, Skipper,' said the loose-forward to the captain after the game. 'I don't know what went wrong – it was such an easy shot! I could kick myself!'

'I shouldn't bother,' said the captain acidly. 'You'd probably miss!'

Did you hear about the paranoid referee who suddenly walked off the pitch in the middle of a match? As he explained to his psychiatrist the following day, 'Every time they went into a scrum, I felt they were all talking about me!'

Rugby Club Riddle

What's the difference between 'Oooooh!' and 'Aaaaah!'?
About four inches.

First girl: **'I hear you're going out with a rugby player. Is he any good in bed?'**
Second girl: **'No, not much. I got him to take some rhino-horn pills.'**
First girl: **'What for?'**
Second girl: **'They're supposed to be an aphrodisiac.'**
First girl: **'Did they do any good?'**
Second girl: **'Yes – but the trouble is that now every time he sees a Land Rover, he charges at it.'**

'Mummy, what's an orgasm?' the team captain's small son asked his mother one morning.

'That's something your father has in the bedroom in thirty seconds,' she replied, 'and I have in the bathroom afterwards.'

A fellow was dancing with a rather haughty partner who was getting increasingly annoyed at his clumsiness.

After stepping on her toes for the third time, he said apologetically, 'Do forgive me. I'm a little stiff from rugby.'

'I don't give a damn where you come from,' she replied. 'This is the last time I'm dancing with you!'

A couple of fans were watching a rugby challenge cup match on a particularly dark and dismal afternoon. Neither team was on top form and the match had rapidly become boring and lifeless. Suddenly the stadium lights flickered and then went out, leaving the pitch in semi-darkness. It was impossible to continue and the match was quickly abandoned.

'Well!' said one fan to his neighbour. 'That's the first time I've ever known bad play stop light!'

A young lady was driving home from a rugby club dance. A patrol officer in a panda car noticed that her vehicle was weaving about all over the road and he pulled her over and gave her the breathalyser test.

Examining the results, he said, 'Madam, I think you've had a couple of stiff ones!'

'Oh!' she replied. 'Does it show that too?'

An elderly rugby referee died and went to purgatory. There he met another old referee, who was walking along arm in arm with a beautiful young Page Three girl.

'Well!' said the old ref, 'I see you're getting your reward up here while you purge your sins.'

'She's not my reward,' said his friend. 'I'm her punishment.'

A fellow went into a pub with his dog. They were both keen supporters of their local rugby team and they watched the Saturday match on TV with great interest. Every time the home team scored a try, the dog barked and yelped with delight.

'What does he do when the other team scores?' asked the barman.

'He does somersaults,' said the dog's owner.

'How many?' asked the barman.

'Depends on how hard I kick him!'

The club manager's wife decided to take a holiday in the sun on her own. At the end of the fortnight, she telephoned her husband and said, 'I'm feeling a new woman – can I stay another week?'

'So am I,' he said. 'Stay as long as you like.'

The club secretary and his wife were making love in bed.

'Am I hurting you?' he asked suddenly.

'No – why do you ask?' said his wife.

'I thought you moved,' he replied.

Fred the Full-back is bisexual. If he can't get any sex, he buys it.

There is a story about an old-time Scottish club manager, Andy McLeish, who was sitting by the bedside of his dying wife one evening.

'Jennie,' he said at last, 'I've got to go – it's an important practice session. If you should feel yourself slipping away while I'm gone, will you please blow out the candle.'

Overhead in the Changing Rooms

What's the worst thing about being an egg? You only get laid once. It takes you ten minutes to get hard. And the only one who sits on your face is your mother.

'I've started going to watch Hull Kingston Rovers.'

'Why?'

'My doctor told me to avoid too much excitement.'

A front-row forward stayed out celebrating with his victorious team until well into the small hours. When he finally made it home, his wife had already gone to bed.

'Is my dinner warm?' he bellowed up the stairs.

'Only if the dustbin's on fire,' she yelled back.

Fred the Full-back tried to have sexual intercourse in his girlfriend's ear because he'd heard that aural sex was fun.

Rugby Club Philosophy

A pregnant woman is a girl who took seriously what was poked at her in fun.

Rugby Club Riddle

What's the definition of a good friend?

Someone who goes into town, gets two blow-jobs, and comes back and gives you one.

When Fred the Full-back was first married, one of his wife's wedding presents was a Polaroid camera. On the first night of the honeymoon, she said, 'I want to take a picture of you in the nude, Fred. Come on!'

When the picture came out of the camera, she took one look at it and said, 'I think I'd better get this enlarged!'

Every speaker at rugby club dinners is fond of sprinkling his speech with a selection of saucy anecdotes. Here are some of the more popular ones heard on these festive occasions:

'Mummy, Mummy, is it a bad thing to have a willy?'

'No, why?'

'Because Daddy is in the bathroom trying to pull his off!'

A fellow came home one evening and said to his wife, 'I've found a great new position for love-making!' 'What is it?' she asked.

'Back to back!' he replied.

'What are you talking about?' she said.

'That's impossible!'

'No, it isn't,' he said. 'I've found another couple who're willing to help out!'

A very well-endowed young lady was trying on an extremely low-cut evening gown in the dress shop. 'What do you think?' she asked the assistant.

'Do you have hair on your chest?' asked the girl.

'No, of course not!' said the customer.

'In that case, the dress is too low-cut!'

A woman went to her doctor and complained about pains in her stomach. The doctor examined her and said, 'You're pregnant.'

'That's impossible!' she said indignantly. 'It must be something in the air!'

'Yes,' said the medic. 'Your legs!'

Did you hear about the girl who sat on Pinocchio's nose and said, 'Tell me a lie. Now tell me the truth. Now tell me a lie . . . ! Now tell me the truth! . . . Now tell me a lie . . . !'?

The groom and his best man were standing together looking round the reception room.

The groom said, 'Do you realise that, except for my sister and my fiancée, I've had every woman here!'

The best man replied, 'Well, between the two of us, we got 'em all!'

A charming young lady was appearing on a television quiz show.

'For £100,' said the quizmaster, 'who was the first man?'

'Adam,' she replied brightly.

'Correct! Now for £500, who was the first woman?'

'Eve,' she said confidently.

'Right!' said the quizmaster. 'Now for £1000 – what was the first thing Eve said to Adam?'

The girl thought for a moment and then said, 'Boy, that's hard!'

'Correct!' said the quizmaster. 'Give the lady the £1000!'

A male squirrel was running frantically around the base of a tree, while a female squirrel flaunted herself tantalisingly on the top branch.

A fellow who was watching said to the squirrel, 'Why don't you go up after her?'

'Listen,' said the squirrel. 'Did you ever try to climb a tree with a hard-on?'

The first young lady to enter the confessional box told the priest that she had allowed a man to fondle her breasts. She was ordered to wash them in holy water. The next young lady confessed that she had touched a man's private parts. The priest told her to wash her hands in holy water. As the two girls were washing in the font, they were joined by a third girl.

'Move over, ladies,' she said. 'I've got to gargle.'

A world-famous surgeon discovered a way to turn women into virgins again. On his first attempt, he took a small piece of the woman's ear and attached it to her pussy. The experiment was a complete failure. But something good came of it – now she can hear herself coming.

A woman went to the doctor and told him she was very worried about the two green spots that had appeared on her inner thighs.

The doctor examined her and said, 'Is your husband a gypsy?'

'Yes, he is,' she said in amazement.

'Well,' said the medic, 'tell him that his earrings aren't made of gold.'

A mouse ran up a girl's leg under her dress and came to rest in her bosom.

'You must be a titmouse,' she said.

'No,' replied the mouse. 'I'm a Mickey Mouse but I overshot the mark.'

A little kid sneaked into a sex show in Soho. Suddenly he ran out in a panic.

'What's the matter with you?' asked the bouncer on the door.

'My mum said if I ever looked at anything bad, I'd turn to stone – and part of me just started!' cried the lad.

First spectator: 'What do you think of our new front row?'
Second spectator: 'I've seen better centres in a box of Black Magic!'

The whole team was surprised when the elderly coach married a sweet young thing of nineteen. On the first night of the honeymoon, she jumped into bed, and the old guy held up five fingers.

'Oh, goody!' she cried. 'Does that mean five times?'

'No,' he said. 'You pick one.'

Rugby Club Riddle

When is it dangerous to have a wet dream?
When you're sleeping under an electric blanket.

The club chairman's wife went to the dentist and as she sat down in the chair, she said, 'I hate coming to the dentist's – I think I'd even rather have a baby!'

And the dentist said, 'Well, make up your mind, so I'll know how to adjust the chair.'

The team captain walked into his teenage son's bedroom one morning and caught the lad playing with himself.

'If you carry on doing that,' he stormed, 'you'll go blind!'

'Can I carry on until I need glasses?' the lad replied.

Rugby Club Philosophy

A contraceptive is an article which should be worn on every conceivable occasion.

They've got a new kind of test now for prospective front-row forwards. They take them down to Selfridges during the January sales, and if they can fight their way through to the counter, they're in!

I belonged to a rugby club once. Our team's expectations were not what you'd call exceptionally high. Our motto was: 'We'll get 'em next time!'

A professional rugby player's little son came home one day after trying out for a junior XV. His father asked him what position he was going to play in.

'I'm not playing in any position,' said the youngster.

'Why not?' asked his father in surprise.

'Well,' said the lad, 'they found out I couldn't run, or tackle, or pass. All I could do was shout and yell. So they made me coach.'

A reporter visited an International full-back in hospital the day after a big match.

'I understand you were the victim of a late tackle,' he said.

'You could call it a late tackle, I suppose,' said the full-back. 'He knocked me down in the bar after the game.'

Rugby Club Riddle

Why has Frankenstein's monster got no children?
Because his nuts are in his neck.

'Little Willy wants to know where he comes from,' said the team captain's wife one evening. 'You're his father – you should tell him.'

The skipper downed a couple of stiff drinks and called little Willy in. For the next half hour, he told him all about the birds and the bees, and then moved on to mummies and daddies . . .

When he finished, he said, 'I hope that's helped you understand, Willy – but, tell me, why did you want to know where you come from?'

'Well,' said the boy, 'I've made friends with this lad at school – and he comes from Birmingham.'

The club secretary's wife went to the optician's for a new pair of spectacles. The optician pointed to the bottom line on his eye-chart and said. 'Can you read this?'

She said, 'No.'

He tried the next line up with the same result. He worked his way up to the largest letters on the top line, without success. Finally, in frustration, he whipped out his dick and said, 'Well, can you see this?'

'Yes,' said the woman.

'Just as I thought,' said the optician. 'You're cock-eyed!'

Fred the Full-back: 'I'd like to try something new. Can we do it doggy-style?'

Fred's girlfriend: 'Well, all right. As long as we choose a street where no one will recognise us!'

A husky young full-back with a lot of surplus energy to work off went into a chemist shop and asked for a powerful aphrodisiac. He explained that he had invited two nymphomaniacs up to his apartment for the night. The next morning, the rugger man staggered into the chemist's and asked for some liniment.

'For your penis?' smiled the chemist.

'No,' he said. 'For my arm. The girls never showed up.'

The front-row forward decided to get a tattoo. 'Any suggestions?' he said to the tattooist.

'Do you love your wife?' he was asked.

'Of course I do,' he replied.

'Well,' said the tattooist, 'why not have "I Love You" tattooed on your penis?'

'Great idea!' said the rugby man. 'Let's go!'

In bed that evening, he threw back the sheets and said to his wife, 'What do you think of that, Love?'

'There you go again!' she said. 'Always trying to put words in my mouth!'

'There's too much gossip in this club,' said the manager to the recently-hired coach. 'I don't want you telling everybody how much you earn here.'

'Don't worry,' said the coach. 'I'm just as ashamed of it as you are.'

A big full-back rather fancied himself as a ladies' man. He took his girlfriend to a hotel for a night of illicit pleasure, and they both removed their clothes.

She took one look at his equipment and said, 'Just who do you expect to satisfy with that?'

'Me!' he grinned.

Rugby Club Philosophy

These days, many nudist clubs hold regular dances, and these have proved to be very popular. There's a good reason for this. The girls like to see what they're up against.

One night, the club secretary took his wife a glass of water and a couple of aspirins.

'What's this for?' she asked in surprise. 'I haven't got a headache.'

And he said, 'Aha!'

A little scrum-half joined a big northern club and found himself dwarfed by the big 200-pounders. Nobody seemed to pay any attention to him and he began to wonder whether he was being deliberately snubbed. He approached the captain and told him of his troubles.

The captain patted him on the shoulder and said, 'Don't worry about it, son. They're not giving you the cold shoulder. They just haven't seen you yet.'

A girl went driving with a hearty young man from the local rugby club. He started to come on to her rather strongly as they were parked in a lay-by and she told him to stop. Somewhat annoyed, he told her to get out of the car and walk home. That night, she wrote in her diary, 'My legs are my best friends.'

The next day, she went out again with another member of the rugby team. Again, the rugger man started to get fresh and again she walked home. That night, she wrote in her diary, 'My legs are still my best friends.'

The following day, she went out with the team captain himself. This time she was overcome by his manly charms – and she didn't have to walk home. That night she wrote in her diary: 'Even the best of friends must part!'

Fred the Full-back was in the back seat of his car one evening, enjoying a few moments of bliss with his girlfriend, when a policeman came up and shone his torch through the window.

'Do you know you're up a cul-de-sac?' said the copper.

'Oh, sorry, officer,' said Fred. 'I thought she was a Roman Catholic!'

A *further selection of Rugby Club Dinner favourites.*

Three women visited the doctor in company with their daughters. The doctor said to the first one, 'I've told you before what your trouble is – too much smoking. Why, you've even named your daughter Virginia!'

Then he turned to the second woman and said, 'And your trouble is you're too fond of the bottle. You're an alcoholic! You've even named your daughter Sherry!'

The third woman turned to her daughter and said, 'Come along, Fanny – I haven't come here to be insulted!'

Two girls went out together one evening on a blind date. One said to the other, 'I'm feeling pretty tired – if we're not in bed by 10.30 tonight, I'm going home!'

Two astronauts, one male and one female, land on Mars. They are surprised to see that the Martians are a highly sophisticated race, with machines for every conceivable purpose. The male astronaut says, 'I suppose you even make babies mechanically!'

'Of course,' says the Martian leader. He turns to one of the complicated machines, presses a button, and a baby drops out. 'That's how we do it,' he says.

'We don't do it that way,' says the astronaut. 'This is how we do it.' And he grabs the female astronaut and proceeds to give a graphic demonstration of how babies are produced on Earth.

When they have finished, the Martian asks, 'So where's the baby?'

'Oh, we have to wait nine months for that,' says the man from Earth.

'Nine months!' says the Martian. 'Then what was all that rush for at the end?'

The gardener at a convent complained to the Mother Superior that he had seen a nun doing press-ups in his vegetable garden.

'Well, that seems harmless enough,' said the Mother Superior.

'Maybe so,' said the gardener, 'but she's ruined my cucumbers!'

There's a new gynaecologist in Harley Street who specializes in fitting gold diaphragms into women patients whose husbands want to come into money.

The young Indian brave wanted to get married.

'Are you experienced in lovemaking?' asked the chief.

'No,' said the brave.

'Go into the woods,' said the chief. 'Find a tree with knot-hole. Get experience.' Two weeks later, the young buck returned.

'I've got experience,' he said. So the chief picked out a beautiful young squaw for him, and the two of them retired to the tepee where they both quickly undressed. Then the young buck told the squaw to turn round and bend over – and when she did so, he kicked her firmly on the backside.

'What did you do that for?' she shrieked.

'I'm not stupid,' said the brave. 'I'm checking for bees!'

A fellow booked into a hotel and was given a room next to a honeymoon couple. Just as he was dropping off to sleep, he heard a man's voice from the next room saying, 'Suck, Doreen, suck! Blowing is just a figure of speech!'

ANDY HUNT

An elephant and a mouse were walking along one day when the elephant suddenly fell into a deep ditch. 'Help!' he shouted. 'Get me out of here!'

'How?' said the mouse. 'I'm too small to pull you out.'

'See that big Mercedes over there?' said the elephant. 'Get the tow rope out of the boot, attach it to the back of the Mercedes, throw down the end of the rope to me, and then drive off and pull me out.'

The mouse did as he was instructed and pulled the elephant out of the ditch. But after getting out of the car, the mouse slipped and fell into the ditch himself.

'Help!' he shouted. 'Get me out of here!'

'How?' said the elephant. 'I'm too big to get into the Mercedes.'

'Well, in that case,' said the mouse, 'just lower your dick down into the ditch and I'll climb up it.'

So the elephant lowered his dick down into the ditch and the mouse climbed out safely. And the moral of the story is: If you've got a big dick, you don't need a Mercedes.

During the war, a fellow who was called up for military service went along for his medical examination. When he'd stripped off, the doctor took one look at his wedding tackle and said, 'You're rather small, aren't you?' And the fellow said, 'We're only going to fight them, aren't we?'

Three sisters were getting ready to go out for the evening. The first one said to her mother, 'I'm going out with Pete to eat.'

'Fine,' said her mother. 'Don't be late home.' The second daughter said, 'I'm going out with Lance to dance.'

'OK,' said her mother. 'Have a nice time.' Then the third daughter said, 'I'm going out with Chuck.'

'You stop where you are!' said the mother. 'You're not going anywhere!'

An elderly Irish priest decided it was time for him to take a holiday, his first in twenty years. So he flew over from Dublin to London and one evening he was taking a stroll through Soho when he was accosted by an attractive young lady who said, 'Hello, dearie! Fancy a quickie? Only £10.'

He continued on his walk, somewhat puzzled, and when he returned to Dublin at the end of his holiday, he said to the Mother Superior, 'Reverend Mother, do you happen to know what a "quickie" is?'

'Sure, Father,' she replied. 'Ten quid – same as London!'

Did you hear about the Irishman who put crushed ice in his condom to keep the swelling down?

A policeman on patrol in Soho late one night shone his torch into a dark doorway and saw a young woman standing there with her skirt up to her waist and her knickers down round her ankles, calmly eating from a bag of chips.

'What's going on here?' asked the policeman.

'Oh!' she said, glancing down. 'Has he gone then?'

Sadie and Mabel went to the cinema and halfway through the film, Sadie whispered, 'Mabel – the chap sitting next to me is masturbating!'

'Take no notice,' Mabel whispered back.

'Yes,' said Sadie, 'but he's using my hand!'

A policeman on his beat came across two men knocking merry hell out of each other. A small boy was watching them with tears streaming down his face, and crying, 'Daddy! Daddy!' in a tremulous voice.

'All right, son, take it easy,' said the policeman. 'Which one is your Daddy?'

'That's what they're fighting about!' sobbed the boy.

'Would you like a blow-job?' said the prostitute to the Irishman.

'Would it affect my unemployment benefit?' he replied.

An old fellow on crutches hobbled up to an ice cream van on the seafront at Brighton and ordered a vanilla sundae.

'Crushed nuts?' asked the salesgirl.

'No,' he said. 'Arthritis.'

Rugby Club Riddle

What's the difference between a virgin and a lightbulb?
You can unscrew a lightbulb.

'When you were on the rugby team, what position did you play in?'

'Bent over like this.'

An Ireland International, well-known for his lack of respect towards referees, went up to one official and asked, 'What would you do if I called you a stupid bastard?'

'What!' said the referee. 'Why I'd book you and send you off, of course!'

'Well, what would you do if I only *thought* you were a stupid bastard?'

'Well,' said the referee doubtfully, 'if you only *thought* it, there's not a lot I could do.'

'In that case,' said the International, 'I think you're a stupid bastard!'

Rugby Club Philosophy

A bisexual is a man who likes girls as well as the next fellow.

The team skipper had a magnificent head of thick black hair. His wife was also a brunette, so when their first baby was born, and it turned out to be a redhead, the skipper began to get worried. He went to the doctor and explained the situation.

'There's never been a redhead in my family,' he said. 'Nor in my wife's family either.'

'How many times do you make love to your wife?' asked the medic.

'Oh, two or three times a year,' said the skipper.

'Ah, well, that's it then,' said the doctor. 'You're rusty!'

Rugby Club Riddle

What's the best thing about self-abuse?

You don't have to look your best.

A North Country rugger man visiting London for an away match went in to Woolworth's and said to one of the salesgirls, 'Do you keep stationery?'

'Well,' she said, 'I do at first, but during the last ten seconds, I just go wild.'

The club secretary's wife was telling her husband about her visit to the doctor. 'Doctor Evans gave me a thorough examination and do you know what? He said I had a beautiful pair of breasts!'

'Oh, yes?' said the club secretary. 'Did he say anything about your big fat arse?'

'I don't think your name ever came up, dear,' she replied.

Gloria, the team mascot, went up to the man behind the counter at her local hardware store and said, 'Will you give me a screw for my cupboard door?'

'OK,' said the salesman. 'And if you're any good, I'll take you out to dinner after.'

Fred the Full-back's girlfriend told him she wanted foreplay so he went out and got three more guys.

The rugby team had been going rapidly downhill and was now in dire financial straits. The club manager came home one evening and said to his wife, 'I think you'd better learn how to cook, my dear, because we're going to have to get rid of cook. And you'd better learn to clean the house, because we'll have to get rid of the cleaning lady.'

'OK,' said his wife, 'but you'd better learn to screw, so we can fire the chauffeur too.'

During a particularly rough game between Wales and Scotland, a Welsh full-back received a severe blow in the privates. His injuries were so severe that he had to have his penis amputated. Through a miracle of medical technology, the surgeons were able to graft on a baby elephant's trunk as a replacement.

After he had recovered from the operation, he met a young woman at a club social and invited her out to dinner at a posh restaurant. Halfway through the meal, the trunk popped out of his pants, reached across the table, grabbed a bread roll, and scooted back again. The girl thought she must be imagining things so she said nothing.

After this had happened three or four times more, however, she said, 'What on earth is that?' The rugger man explained.

'That's amazing!' she exclaimed. 'Can you make it do it again?'

'Yes, I think so,' said the full-back. 'But to tell you the truth, I don't think my arse could take another bread roll!'

The coach's little boy walked into the bedroom and saw that his father was holding a condom. 'What's that, Daddy?' he asked.

'Oh, it's – er – I'm just going to catch a moth, son,' said the coach.

'And after you catch it,' said the youngster, 'what are you going to do with it – fuck it?'

The wife of a famous All-England rugby player was suing for divorce on the grounds that he was too uncultured and slobbish to live with.

'Whenever we go into a restaurant,' she explained to the lawyer, 'he always drinks his coffee with his pinkie sticking out.'

'Well, that sounds harmless,' said the lawyer. 'Lots of people drink their coffee with their little finger sticking out.'

'Who said anything about his little finger?' she replied.

Fred the Full-back invited his girlfriend over to his apartment to spend the night in dalliance. As they prepared for bed, he said, 'Honey, I'm going to screw you like you've never been screwed before!' Half an hour later, she pulled a feather out of the pillow and started to tap him on the head with it.

'What are you doing, honey?' he asked.

'Well,' she said, 'comparatively speaking, I'm beating your brains out!'

Two members of the local rugby team who were close friends were taking a holiday together with their respective wives. After a week at the seaside they were both thoroughly bored. In the bar one night they decided to exchange partners in order to see if they could liven up the holiday. The following morning at breakfast they compared notes.

'I'm glad we tried that,' said one. 'I had a smashing time! Ah, here come the girls. Let's ask them how they got on.'

When the retired referee finally passed on, his wife arranged for him to be cremated. When the undertaker asked her what sort of an urn she wanted for the ashes, she said, 'Never mind about that. Just put them into this paper bag.'

The undertaker thought this rather a strange request, but he did as she asked, and she carried the bag home and went straight into the bedroom. Then she turned down the lights, put on a romantic record, and tipped the ashes into her hands. 'Here you are, Norman – here's that blow-job you were always asking me for!' – and blew the ashes all over the bed.

The club chairman's wife was playing with his penis.

'Darling, didn't you tell me once that you were the only man who had one of these?' she asked.

'That's right, dear,' said her husband.

'Well, do you know, I found out yesterday that the team captain has one too!'

'Ah . . . yes . . .' said the club chairman. 'Well, that's because I had a spare one, you see – and I gave it to him.'

'Well, that was silly of you,' replied his wife. 'You gave the best and biggest one away!'

Rugger man: 'Am I the first fellow to sleep with you?'
Girlfriend: 'Yes, all the others stayed awake!'

The roughest, toughest front-row forward in the team walked into a pub one night with a crocodile on a lead. He hit the crocodile over the head with a lager bottle and it opened its mouth wide and appeared to pass out. Then the rugby man whipped out his dick and stuck it in the crocodile's mouth, pulling it out just in time before the creature's jaws snapped shut again.

'Now then,' he bellowed, looking around at the assembled customers, 'is there anyone in this pub tonight with the courage to do that?'

A little old lady in the corner stood up and said, 'I don't mind having a go – but don't hit me too hard with the bottle.'

A man was watching a Stones Super League Final when another chap approached him and said, 'Excuse me, is this seat taken?'

'No – help yourself,' said the first spectator. 'I expected it to be taken when I bought the tickets, but all my mates are at the wife's funeral.'

The local rugby team captain was in the pub one night when he noticed the landlord's dog behind the bar counter, contentedly licking its balls. He laughed and said to the landlord, 'I wish *I* could do that!'

'Well,' said the landlord, 'give him a biscuit and he might let you.'

The match was rained off just before half-time and the referee returned home a couple of hours before he was expected. He went into the bedroom and found a stranger in bed with his wife, with his head cradled between her breasts.

'What the hell's going on here?' he shouted.

'I'm listening to the music,' said the stranger.

'You're what!' said the ref. 'Get out of it! Let me have a listen!' He bent over and put his head on his wife's chest. 'I can't hear any music,' he said suspiciously.

'Of course you can't,' said the stranger. 'You're not plugged in!'

Rugby Club Riddle

Give me an example of something really brave and courageous.

Two cannibals having oral sex.

The wife of a very famous England team captain, whose current line-up included a large number of players with distinctly un-English names like Panatelli, Uzbecki and Rochefoucauld, went to the doctor one day with 'woman's trouble'.

The doctor examined her and asked, 'When did you last have a check-up?'

'I don't think I ever had,' she replied. 'I've had an Italian, a Romanian, a Frenchman . . .'

Girlfriend: 'Fred, you may be a good full-back, but you're a lousy lover!'
Fred: 'How can you tell in ten seconds?'

The coach burst into the changing room as the second half of the game was about to begin.

'All right!' he roared. 'All of you lazy, no-good, thick-headed bastards – out on that field – now!' All the players jumped to their feet and rushed out onto the field – except for the little scrum-half sitting in the corner.

'Well!' roared the coach.

'Well!' said the little scrum-half. 'There certainly were a lot of them, weren't there!'

The team captain's little boy was passing his parents' bedroom one evening when they happened to be in bed together. He glanced in and stared for a moment.

'Well!' he said. 'And you have the nerve to slap me for sucking my thumb!'

The club manager's wife was rushed to hospital and he went with her in the ambulance. After waiting for half an hour, the doctor emerged from the examination room and said, 'Your wife has acute angina.'

'Yes, I know that,' said the club manager. 'But what's wrong with her?'

Rugby Club Riddle

Why did the Irish International always wear two condoms? To be sure, to be sure.

Scrum-half: 'How many kids have you got?'
Full-back: 'Fourteen – all boys.'
Scrum-half: 'One more and you'll have your own rugby team!'
Full-back: 'How many kids have you got?'
Scrum-half: 'Seventeen – all girls.'
Full-back: 'One more and you'll have your own golf-course!'

The team skipper ran into an old mate in the pub and they stayed drinking until quite late.

'You'd better come and spend the night at my house,' said the skipper. 'You'll have to sleep with my brother-in-law, and I must warn you – he snores! I hope he won't keep you awake.'

The next morning, when his mate came down to breakfast, the skipper said, 'How did you sleep?'

'Fine,' said his friend. 'I slept like a log all night.'

'Didn't my brother-in-law's snoring keep you awake?' asked the captain.

'No,' came the reply. 'Just before we put out the light, I kissed him on the cheek and said, "Sleep tight, honey-bun!" He never closed his eyes all night.'

Rugby Club Philosophy

A gay masochist is what you might call a sucker for punishment.

The rugby club were throwing a big party one Saturday night at the clubhouse, and all the players and officials were there with their wives and girlfriends. The club chairman turned up late and found a boisterous game in full swing.

'Come on, boss,' urged the team captain. 'This is fun! We've blindfolded all the girls and now they're trying to identify the men by feeling their private parts!'

'Disgusting!' said the chairman. 'I'm not taking part in a game like that!'

'You might as well,' said the skipper. 'Your name's been guessed three times already!'

Overheard in the Changing Room

A woman walked into a butcher's shop in Manchester and said to the bloke behind the counter, 'Do you keep dripping?'

'Yes, I do,' said the butcher.

'Me too,' she said. 'Embarrassing, isn't it?'

Did you hear about the man who had five pricks? His pants fitted him like a glove.

A man had been riding through the Sahara Desert for a week, and he began to get extremely horny. He dismounted, backed the camel over to a pile of rocks, climbed on top of the pile, and unzipped his flies.

Immediately, the camel took a few steps forward, out of reach.

He got down, backed the camel up, and tried again – with the same result. This went on several times when suddenly a beautiful young woman walked up.

The man eyed her up and down, and then said, 'Excuse me, miss – would you mind holding my camel?'

Two cannibals were sitting in the middle of the jungle. One had a glossy magazine, and he was tearing out pictures of men and women, and stuffing them into his mouth.

'Tell me,' said the second cannibal. 'Is that dehydrated stuff any good?'

An old fellow of about eighty-five was sitting in the pub one evening when a chap came up to him and said, 'Pardon me, but didn't you used to be a strong man at the circus? If I remember rightly, you used to have an act where you bent a great big iron bar over your prick.'

'That's right,' said the old codger. 'Mind you, I can't do that any more. My wrists have gone.'

The vicar had just got married to a nubile young girl of the parish. He went into the bathroom to undress and when he re-entered the bedroom, there was his bride lying on the bed, stark naked, and with her legs spread wide.

'Really, my dear,' said the vicar, somewhat shocked. 'I expected to find you on your knees by the side of the bed.'

'Well, all right, if that's how you want it,' she said. 'But I must warn you – it gives me hiccups!'

Did you hear about the deaf gynaecologist?
He had to learn how to read lips.

'Daddy,' said a small child to his father, 'what's a transvestite?'

'Don't ask me,' replied his dad. 'Ask your mother – he's in the kitchen.'

'Son, I have something to tell you,' said the fond father. 'The stork is going to bring you a little baby brother any day now!'

'Blimey!' said the kid. 'Mum said there was going to be a new baby under the gooseberry bush – and Grandma said the doctor was going to be bringing one in his little black bag! The place is going to be overrun with bloody kids!'

A young nun requested an interview with the Mother Superior and confessed that she was pregnant.

'What!' exclaimed the Reverend Mother. 'How did this happen? Who was the man?'

'It wasn't a man, Reverend Mother, it was an angel from above,' said the nun.

'What are you talking about?' said the Mother Superior. 'How do you know he was an angel?'

'I saw his name inside his vest,' said the nun. 'Saint Michael!'

An old fellow of eighty-seven married a young lass of twenty. Eight months later, the old boy went round to see the vicar to arrange for a christening. The vicar was amazed.

'Well!' he said. 'A christening, eh? And at your age! Congratulations! So you're starting another family then.'

'No – this'll be the last,' said the old man. 'My grown-up son's leaving for America next week.'

A dark suspicion began to grow in the vicar's mind. 'Oh, yes?' he said. 'And what's your grown-up son got to do with it?'

'Well,' said the old boy, 'he used to lift me on and off.'

At a recent wedding at our local church, the bride was heavily pregnant, so the guests threw puffed rice.

Two fellows were sitting together on a train and one of them was continually scratching his elbow. At the next station, the elbow-scratcher got out, and a man sitting opposite said to his friend, 'That's an irritating habit your mate's got – scratching away at his elbow all the time.'

'Yes,' was the reply. 'He's got a nasty case of piles.'

'Piles?' said the stranger. 'What's that got to do with his elbow?'

'Well, you see, he's a Conservative politician – he can't tell his arse from his elbow.'

'I want to go to the loo,' a little boy said to his mother.

'Well, I'm too busy now,' she replied. 'Ask your grandad to take you.'

'I'd rather ask Grandma,' said the little lad. 'Her hand shakes more.'

Full-back: 'Did you take my advice about kissing your girlfriend when she least expected it?'

Scrum-half: '*When* she least expected it? I thought you said *where*!'

Rugby Club Riddle

Why do eunuchs wear their underpants when they're taking a shower?

They hate to look down on the unemployed.

A rugby man travelled down to London from the north for an important away match and decided to spend the night in a hotel after the game. When he returned home the next day, his wife told him that, during the night, a burglar had paid them a visit.

'My God!' said the rugger man. 'Did he get anything?'

'I'll say!' said the wife. 'In the dark, I thought he was you!'

Snow White arrived home one evening to find her house destroyed by fire. She was doubly worried because she'd left all seven dwarfs sleeping inside. As she scrambled through the wreckage, frantically calling their names, she suddenly heard a voice cry: 'England for the Triple Crown!'

'Thank goodness,' she sobbed. 'At least Dopey's still alive!'

One of the coaching staff came home early from a practice session to find the team doctor in bed with his wife.

'What the hell do you think you're doing?' he stormed.

'I'm . . . er . . . I'm . . . taking your wife's temperature,' stammered the medic.

'Right!' said the coach. 'I hope for your sake that thing's got numbers on it when you take it out!'

A favourite toast at rugby club dinners is: 'Here's to the kisses we've snatched – and vice versa!'

The three daughters of the managing director of a rugby club all got married on the same day, and they all spent the first night, with their husbands, as guests of their father in his palatial Hampstead home. Towards midnight, the parents began to wonder how their daughters were getting on, so they crept upstairs and listened outside each door in turn.

Through door number one, they heard the first daughter laughing her head off; through door number two, they heard the second daughter crying her eyes out; but when they listened at the third door, there wasn't a sound to be heard.

The next day, the parents took their daughters to one side and asked for an explanation.

The first daughter said, 'Well, you always told me to laugh when I was being tickled.'

The second daughter said, 'And you always told me to cry when I was hurt.'

And the third daughter said, 'You always told me never to talk with my mouth full.'

Every club chairman worth his salt has a fund of favourite anecdotes which he regularly trots out at the annual club dinner and dance. Here is a selection from the more popular repertoires.

Did you hear about the FBI agent in America who was ordered to shadow one of the leaders of the Gay Liberation Movement? He blew his assignment.

A woman discovered a dead cat in her garden, so she bundled it up in a bag and caught a bus out of town, telling the driver that she wanted to dump the cat in the woods out in the country.

By the time the bus reached the woods, it was permeated with the stink of the animal's dead body. The driver was pretty fed up by this time, and he shouted, 'Will the lady with the stinking pussy get off now please!' Three women crossed their legs, and two got off the bus in a huff!

Two farmers were talking in the pub one evening. 'I hear you gave your sheep some of them special sex pills to make 'em breed better,' said one. 'What's in 'em?'

'I don't rightly know,' said the other farmer. 'But they taste of peppermint.'

A little brother and sister were playing in the garden, and as it was a very hot summer's day, and the sun was blazing down, they decided to take off all their clothes.

Seconds later, the little girl ran into the house crying, and said, 'Mummy, Tommy's got something I haven't got, between his legs!'

'Don't worry, dear,' said her mother. 'As long as you've got one of *those*, you'll be able to get plenty of *them* when you grow up!'

An American was making his first visit to London. He met a hooker in a pub one night and fell into conversation with her.

'You know, honey,' he said, 'I come from the other side.'

'Let's go back to my place,' she said. 'This I've got to see!'

A Conservative politician got married to a girl who was a staunch Labour supporter. On the first night of the honeymoon, they started to argue about politics, and the dispute continued until they had got into bed and turned out the lights.

After about ten minutes, the girl said, 'Darling, there's a split in the Labour Party, and I think if the Conservative member stood now, he'd get in easily.'

'Too late!' said the Tory. 'He's already stood as an independent, and lost his deposit!'

A woman went into a greengrocer's shop and started examining the cucumbers on display. She picked one up and ran her hand along it, then put it down and picked another one up, and this went on for several minutes until at last the greengrocer said, 'Make up your mind, Lady! They're not like your old man's, you know – they don't get any bigger if you play with them!'

Two old maids paid a visit to the British Museum. When they came to the room devoted to ancient Greek sculpture, the first thing they noticed was a life-sized statue of a handsome young Greek god, entirely naked except for a strategic fig leaf which barely covered his requirements.

One of the old dears was anxious to move on, but the other one stood transfixed to the spot, gazing at the statue.

'Come on, Mabel,' said her friend. 'What are you waiting for – Christmas?'

'No,' said Mabel. 'Autumn!'

A psychiatrist at a London teaching college was giving a lecture on mental health. 'One form of mental illness,' he said to the assembled crowd of students, 'takes the form of a kind of dementia. One moment, the sufferer is rushing around shouting and screaming, and the next moment, he is sitting with his head in his hands, weeping uncontrollably. Now can anyone tell me what is the technical term for that sort of aberration?'

A voice from the back of the hall said confidently, 'A rugby manager!'

Rugby Club Philosophy

The perfect lover is said to be a rugby player with a nine-inch tongue and the ability to breathe through his ears.

The manager of a northern rugby club was watching one of his new players in action. The player didn't make a single pass all afternoon, preferring to keep the ball to himself, usually with disastrous results. Finally the manager muttered to the coach, 'We'll have to change the rules for this chap. We'll have to play with two balls – one for him and one for the rest of the team.'

The brand new centre-forward was proving to be a big disappointment and the coach went up to him at half-time and said, 'The manager's going to pull you off at half-time.'

'Great!' said the new man. 'We only got oranges at my old club!'

Little Bobby, the coach's son, walked into the bathroom one evening, and surprised his mother soaking in the tub.

'What's that, Mummy?' he asked innocently, pointing between her legs.

'Oh,' she said, 'well . . . . that's where your father accidentally kicked me one day.'

'Well!' said little Bobby. 'Fancy that! Got you right in the pussy, eh!'

Fred the Full-back's girlfriend asked him to kiss her somewhere dirty – so he drove her to Oldham.

A member of the Wigan RFC XV, a chap who always looked on the bright side of every misfortune, announced to his team-mates that he was going to be married.

'Who's the lucky girl?' asked one of his mates. 'Sharon Goodbody,' he said proudly.

'You're not going to marry Sharon Goodbody!' said his mate. 'She's been laid by everybody in Wigan!'

'Well,' said the newly-engaged player, 'Wigan's not *that* big a place.'

Sammy the Scrum-half was courting and one evening he took his fiancée out for a walk. They were looking for a quiet spot in which to indulge in a little horizontal jogging, and they came to the local park which, unfortunately, was locked up for the night.

Sammy's girl looked up doubtfully at the high surrounding wall and said, 'How are we going to get over?' Sammy unzipped his flies and took out his proudly erect manhood.

'No problem, love,' he said. 'You just stand on this!'

'That's all very well,' she said. 'But how am I going to get back?'

You may be interested to know that I've just been approached to sign up with a big super league club. I'm a bit worried about the contract though. The first clause forbids me to read any of the other clauses.

Rugby Club Riddle

What's the difference between a David Copperfield magic show and a brothel?

A David Copperfield magic show is full of cunning stunts . . .

Fred the Full-back was once engaged to a lady contortionist from the circus but she broke it off.

Gloria, the team mascot, once went off on a cruise to the West Indies. She kept a diary of events and on the first night, she wrote: 'Met the captain.' On the second night, she wrote: 'Dined at the captain's table.' The third night's entry was: 'The captain appears to be very interested in me.' On the fourth night, she wrote: 'The captain says he is madly in love with me, and swears that if I won't sleep with him, he'll run the ship into an iceberg and sink her.' The final entry in the diary was: 'Tonight I saved the lives of 850 passengers.'

Fred the Full-back was having sex with his girlfriend on the river bank. When they had finished, she said, 'Fred, darling, if anything goes wrong and we have a baby boy, what shall we call him?' Fred tied a knot in the condom, threw it into the river, and said, 'If he gets out of that, we'll call him Houdini!'

Looking around at all the famous rugby coaches milling around in the lobby of the Hilton Hotel during a big IRFB reception, one of the coaches, who had a pretty high opinion of his own superiority, turned to his neighbour, a famous sports editor, and said, 'How many really great coaches do you think there are in this room?' 'One less than you think,' replied the editor.

Two girls were talking about the various dates they had had with the members of the local rugby team.

'I've been out with all of them,' said the first girl. 'But I haven't let one of them make love to me.'

'Oh?' said her friend. 'Which one was that?'

Sammy the Scrum-half got married but, unusually for a rugby player, he was completely innocent, and so he asked his mother on the wedding day, 'I know there's something I'm supposed to do when I get into bed with Sharon tonight, but I'm not quite sure what it is.'

'Well, son,' said his mother, 'you simply put your . . . you know . . . the hardest part of yourself into her . . . into the place where she wee-wees.'

At the honeymoon hotel that night, they had to call for an ambulance. Sammy had got his head stuck in a chamber pot.

A young lady was due to set off for an interview for the position of personal secretary to the rugby club's managing director.

'A word of warning,' said her flatmate. 'This guy has a very bad reputation. Once he gets you alone in his office, he's quite capable of grabbing you and ripping your dress off.'

'Thanks for telling me,' said her friend. 'I'd better go and change into an old one.'

Fred the Full-back went to his optician and asked for a new pair of spectacles. 'I broke my last pair in an accident,' he said.

'What sort of an accident?' asked the optician. 'You don't wear your glasses when you're playing, surely?'

'No,' said Fred. 'You see, I was kissing my girlfriend and . . .'

'How could you break your glasses kissing your girlfriend?' said the optician.

'Well,' said Fred. 'She crossed her legs.'

Fred the Full-back was lying in bed with his girlfriend one night when she suddenly said, 'Well – aren't you going to do something?'

'I'm sorry, sweetheart,' said Fred. 'I'm just too tired to think of anyone.'

The first time Gloria, the team mascot, went off to a swinging holiday camp in the Mediterranean, her father warned her against the predatory young men who would be after her virtue.

'Don't worry, Dad,' she said, tapping her forehead. 'I've got it up here!'

'I don't care where you've got it,' said her father. 'Wherever it is, those randy young buggers will find it!'

The club treasurer's wife was unfortunately involved in a motoring accident which left her face badly cut and bruised. The treasurer consulted a plastic surgeon who said it would certainly be possible to carry out a skin-grafting operation to cover the damage, and suggested that the best way to proceed would be take some skin from the husband's backside. He readily agreed to this, and some weeks after the operation, which was completely successful, the treasurer happened to be talking to the club chairman who naturally asked him all about it.

'There was nothing to it,' said the treasurer. 'And the best thing about it all is the sheer pleasure I get out of watching my mother-in-law kiss my arse!'

Rugby Club Riddle

If the stork brings babies, and larks bring illegitimate babies, what kind of birds don't bring any babies at all?

Swallows.

A selection of favourites from the Team Captain's little blue book of jokes.

All the great comic book heroes decided to hold a beach party. Superman arrived an hour late, with a black eye, a split lip, and his clothes all torn.

The Incredible Hulk said, 'What happened to you, Superman?'

'Well,' said Superman, 'I was flying along down the beach when suddenly I looked down and there was Wonderwoman lying there, completely naked, with her legs spread wide! I figured this opportunity was too good to miss, so I dived straight down – and straight in!'

'I bet she was surprised,' said the Incredible Hulk.

'Yes, she was,' said Superman. 'But not half as surprised as the Invisible Man!'

'How does your husband like that new toilet brush you bought last week?'

'He doesn't mind it but he still prefers to use paper.'

A young office worker in the City told his boss that his wife was going to have a baby, and asked for the day off. The next morning, his boss said, 'Was it a boy or a girl?'

'Oh, it's much too soon to tell,' said the young clerk. 'We have to wait for nine months to find that out.'

'It's my husband,' sobbed the young bride to the marriage guidance counsellor. 'On the first night of the honeymoon, we went to a hotel and when we got into the bedroom, I took off all my clothes, he took off all his clothes, then he put on all my clothes, went out, and I haven't seen him since!'

A very innocent young girl got married and on the first night of the honeymoon, she was too embarrassed to talk about what she was supposed to do. Her husband was very considerate and he explained as tactfully as he could.

'There's no need to say anything,' he said. 'When you want it, just pull it once. If you don't want it, pull it about thirty or forty times.'

A young girl had just got married and one day she was telling her neighbour how she had been teaching her rather uncouth husband some manners.

Just then the husband rushed into the room and said, 'How about a fuck?' The neighbour was shocked.

'I thought you said you had been teaching your husband manners,' she said.

'Oh, yes,' said the young bride. 'A week ago, he wouldn't have asked!'

Gloria, the team mascot, once worked as a chambermaid in a small hotel. One evening, a guest in a room on the top floor, rang the bell for service. When Gloria entered the room, he threw her down on the bed, ripped off all her clothes, and had his way with her.

'And to this day,' says Gloria, 'I never did find out what he rang the bell for.'

Fred the Full-back was wrapped in a passionate embrace with his girlfriend when suddenly they heard the sound of the front door opening.

'Quick,' said the girl. 'It's my husband! He's an all-in wrestler and he's six foot four and weighs 300 pounds!'

'Where's your back door?' said Fred in a panic.

'We haven't got one,' she said.

'Well,' said Fred, 'where would you like one?'

Rugby Club Riddle

Why do women parachutists wear jockstraps?
To stop them whistling on the way down.

The club chairman engaged a nubile young secretary and became smitten by her charms. One day he told her he wanted some old-fashioned loving, so she introduced him to her grandmother.

Mention has been made in these annals of Gloria, the team mascot. Just to fill in the background, here are a few biographical details.

Gloria is all in favour of the Women's Movement. She thinks it's unsporting just to lie there and do nothing.

Gloria goes to the dentist regularly. There's nothing wrong with her teeth. She just loves it when he says, 'Open wide!'

Gloria is an excellent swimmer. And so she should be – she used to be a streetwalker in Venice.

She turned up at work one morning with no make-up, bags under her eyes, and every sign of having had a very rough night.

'You look tired this morning,' said her friend.

'Yeah,' said Gloria. 'I went out on a double date last night and the other girl didn't show up!'

Gloria was once asked whether she had ever been picked up by the fuzz.

'No,' she said, 'but I've been swung round by the tits a few times!'

Gloria has a magnificent mane of blonde hair, but on one occasion (due to an oversight on her part), she gave birth to a baby with bright red hair.

'Did the father have red hair?' asked the obstetrician.

'I don't know,' she said. 'He didn't take his hat off.'

Gloria's friend, Tracey, had just come back from her honeymoon, and was telling Gloria all about it.

'As soon as we got to the hotel,' she said, 'we went up to the bedroom and had a performance. Then we went down to dinner, went upstairs again, and had another performance. Then we went down to the bar for a few drinks, came back to the bedroom, and had another performance. And all through the night it was just performance after performance! Then when we woke up in the morning, we had a dress rehearsal.'

'What's a dress rehearsal?' asked Gloria.

'Oh, it's the same as a performance,' said Tracey, 'but nobody comes.'

NO MORE!!
BRAVO!!
MORE!!
ENCORE!!
MORE!
BRAVO!!
GIVE ME A CALL
GREAT PERFORMANCE LOVE, MUM & DAD

She once said that the reason she keeps dating chemists, biologists and mathematicians is she likes to feel she's giving her body to science.

Gloria once went to the doctor and complained about the bruises on her knees.

'How did you get those?' asked the doctor.

'Well,' she said, 'it's the way we make love. You see, I like to do it doggy-fashion.'

'Well, you'll just have to adopt a more orthodox position,' said the doctor.

'Oh, I couldn't do that,' said Gloria. 'My dog's breath is murder!'

Gloria and her new boyfriend drove out into the countryside, looking for a quiet place for a little horizontal jogging. They found a suitable spot not far from the road, and the boyfriend quickly divested Gloria of her clothes. He had just removed her panties when the sound of a police car could be heard approaching.

'Fuzz!' he whispered excitedly.

'Well, what did you expect?' said Gloria. 'Feathers?'

Full-back: 'I've got an idea of how to improve the game.'
Manager: 'Great! When are you thinking of leaving?'

At the rugby club dinner, the elderly chairman droned on and on, boring everyone to tears with his long-winded and totally unfunny speech. The club treasurer nudged the team captain and said, 'I wish there was a way to shut him up.'

'Leave it to me,' said the skipper. He scribbled a note on a paper napkin and passed it up to the chairman, who read it, quickly finished his speech, and sat down.

'Brilliant!' said the club treasurer. 'What did you put in that note?'

'I just wrote: "Your flies are undone",' said the team captain.

The full-back stormed into the coach's office and raged, 'If the manager doesn't take back what he just said to me, I'm leaving the club!'

'What did he say?' asked the amazed coach.

'He said, "You're fired!"'

During one big match, the coach turned to me and said, 'Phillips – get in there and fight!' So I went in and hit the referee.

Rugby Club Riddle

How can you tell if you're in a gay church?
Only half the congregation are kneeling.

Wally, the Wing-three-quarter, was accosted by a prostitute one evening. She said, 'Hello, honey – shall we get together and have some fun?'

'Sure,' said Wally – so he took her round to his place and they spent the evening playing Monopoly.

Rugby Club Philosophy

Can a lecture on sexual techniques be described as a 'Sermon on the Mount'?

Wally, the Wing-three-quarter, badly needed a holiday and he thought he'd try somewhere different. He settled on Israel as he'd never been there, and booked a fortnight in Tel Aviv.

Walking along the main street one day, he noticed a shop window full of TV sets, radios and video recorders. He needed a new transistor radio so he went into the shop and asked to see some samples.

'We don't sell radios, or anything like that,' said the elderly Jewish shopkeeper. 'We do circumcisions for bar-mitzvahs.'

'But you've got dozens of radios in the window,' protested Wally.

'So what do you want I should put in the window?' said the shopkeeper.

I'll never forget my first game of rugby. The crowd jeered and booed and hissed. But through all the noise, I could hear a voice shouting, 'Give him a chance! Give him a chance!' Then they threw my mother out.

'How's your husband?'

'He's laid up in bed with a rugby injury.'

'I didn't know he played.'

'He doesn't. He sprained his larynx at the match last Saturday.'

Rugby Club Riddle

What do you call a man who marries another man?

A vicar.

A selection of Fred the Full-back's Favourite Jokes:

A prostitute went into a department store and stopped at the cosmetics counter. She asked what perfumes they had in stock and the salesgirl said, 'We've got a very nice one here, madam – it's called "Surrender".'

'Surrender?' said the prostitute. 'I don't want to surrender, dearie – I just want to negotiate a little!'

A beautiful young lady, enjoying a cruise in the south Pacific, had the misfortune to fall overboard one morning. No one noticed the accident, but luckily there was a small island close at hand and she managed to swim ashore.

The only inhabitant was a well-built young man and she asked him how long he had been on the island.

'I don't know,' he said. 'I was shipwrecked when I was a small boy, and I've been here ever since.'

'And you've managed to exist all this time alone?' she said.

'Oh, yes,' he replied. 'I spend hours every day digging for clams on the beach.'

'And what do you do for sex?' she asked, eyeing his magnificent physique.

'Sex?' he said. 'What's that?'

'You mean you don't know what sex is?' she said. 'Come here – I'll show you.'

Half an hour later she said, 'That's sex. How did you like it?'

'It's all right, I suppose,' said the young man. 'But just look what you've done to my clam-digger!'

A young woman was pushing her baby in a pram through the park and she fell into conversation with an old fellow who congratulated her on her bonny child.

'Yes,' she said, 'and I had begun to think I'd never be a mother. Ten years we've been married, and we tried and tried for a child without success. And now – well, there he is – a beautiful baby boy!'

'Well, persistence will do it every time,' said the old fellow. 'Look at me – I breed pigeons, and for years I never won a race, but now I'm winning prizes and cups all the time.'

'How did you manage it?' asked the young mother.

'I changed the cock,' he replied.

'Why, that's exactly what I did!' she said.

You may be interested to know that I've just signed a contract with St Helens RFC. All I've got to do now is get St Helen's RFC to sign it.

During one International match, the referee found himself constantly being barracked by one particular member of the crowd. When this spectator shouted, 'Oi, ref – that was a foul! Are you blind or something!' the referee strode over to the stands and said, 'What did you say just then?' 'Blimey!' said the spectator, 'he's not only blind – he's deaf as well!'

A North Country club engaged the services of a massive 280-pound front-row forward whose only drawback was that he was rather slow. At a match one Saturday afternoon, this monster was standing motionless in the middle of the pitch, apparently in a trance.

'Oi, Jenkins!' the coach shouted from the touch-line. 'Move around a bit! You're killing the grass!'

The team captain took Wally, the Wing-three-quarter, aside one day and said, 'I'm sorry to tell you this, Wally, but I think your wife's being unfaithful to you.'

'I don't believe it,' said Wally. 'Not Louise. I'm sure you're wrong.'

'Well, I'm sure I'm right,' said the skipper. 'But why don't you find out for yourself? Go home early today, before she's expecting you.'

'I'll do that,' said Wally. 'But I'm sure you're wrong.'

The next day, the team captain said, 'Did you take my advice?'

'Yes,' said Wally. 'I went home early yesterday, let myself in quietly, tiptoed upstairs, and peeped through the keyhole of the bedroom door. There was my wife, naked on the bed, and there was a strange man undressing. Then he switched off the lights and it was so dark, I couldn't see what happened next. Pity – now we'll never know if I was right or you were.'

Rugby Club Riddle

What is the definition of unskilled labour?
A pregnant prostitute.

Did you know that Wally, the Wing-three-quarter, is so lazy, he got himself engaged to a pregnant woman?

The manager of a lowly London and South-east rugby club took his team on an African safari holiday, and while there, he came across a native athlete who could run, kick, pass, and juggle a coconut like a born rugby player.

Excitedly, the manager called a meeting of all the players and introduced the young athlete to them. 'This fellow's brilliant!' he said, 'and I've persuaded him to join the team, on six months' trial. His name is Obongo Matabulu. Now then,' he continued, holding up a rugby ball, 'this – ball – BALL!' Then, pointing at the goalposts, he said, 'That – goal – GOAL! That – goal line – GOAL LINE! You put BALL over GOAL LINE: or kick BALL over CROSSBAR.'

'You don't need to explain the game in those simple and rather patronising terms, old boy,' said Obongo Matabulu. 'I played for Harrow when I went to school there, and later for the Cambridge University XV.'

'I'm not talking to you,' said the manager. 'I'm talking to the rest of the team!'

At one Saturday afternoon match, I thought we were in with a good chance of winning. Then the match started . . .

Rugby Club Philosophy

A nudist camp is a place where men and women go to air their differences.

A traffic policeman stopped a drunken driver and asked him to blow into the bag. The driver promptly handed him a card which said: ASTHMATIC: DON'T TAKE BREATH SAMPLES.

The policeman said in that case, he would take a blood sample, whereupon the driver handed over another card which read: HAEMOPHILIAC: DON'T TAKE BLOOD SAMPLES.

By this time the policeman was getting somewhat annoyed, so he demanded a urine sample. The driver produced a third card which read: DEWSBURY MOOR RFC: SUPPORTERS CLUB: DON'T TAKE THE PISS.

Rugby Club Philosophy

One of the most controversial questions of modern times is: Do test tubes need foreplay?

The chairman of a Pennine League club was retiring after many years of loyal service. At the dinner given in his honour by the club, the team captain, who had 'the drink taken', as they say in Ireland, rose to make his speech.

'It is said,' he began, 'that when a child is born, its guardian angel gives it a kiss. If the kiss is on the hands, the child will become a musician or an artist. If the kiss is on the head, it will become a great thinker or scientist. If on the lips, it will grow up to be a singer or an actor. Now I don't know where our Charlie here was kissed, but he's certainly been a damn good chairman!'

Rugby Club Philosophy

Masturbation can best be described as a sort of self-service elevator.

Gloria, the team mascot, also has a collection of favourite stories, of which the following is a small selection. (By the way, Gloria's favourite colour is blue!)

Two prostitutes were chatting and one said, 'How's business been today?'

'Great!' said the other one. 'I've been up and down those stairs fifty-six times today!'

'Oh!' said the first hooker. 'Your poor feet!'

A young man at a nudist camp said to a girl, 'Why do you lower your eyes when I say I love you?'

'To see if it's true,' she replied.

A pianist applied for a job in the cocktail lounge of a very high-class hotel in the West End of London. The hotel manager said, 'You'll need to wear a dinner suit.'

'I'm afraid I haven't got one,' said the pianist.

'Well, I can lend you a second-hand one,' said the manager. 'It's a bit tatty but it'll be all right if you don't stand up. Oh, and one other thing – we often get requests for songs from the customers – can you handle that?'

'No problem,' said the pianist. 'Anything you can hum, I can play.'

All went well on the first evening, but when the customers applauded, the pianist inadvertently stood up to take a bow. The manager, who was standing nearby, said, 'Sit down! Do you know your balls are hanging out!' And the pianist said, 'You hum it, I'll play it!'

Two gays were having a terrible row. 'Drop dead!' the first one screamed.

'Go to hell!' shrieked his mate.

'Kiss my arse!' said the first one.

'Oh – do you want to make up?' smiled his friend.

As the fat woman said to the fat man: 'Thanks for the tip!'

The lady of the house was instructing the new and rather inexperienced maid about her duties at the big dinner party that was to take place that evening.

'Now, Mary,' she said, 'please make sure that you don't forget to put out the sugar tongs. It's not very nice when the gentlemen have to go to the toilet, and take themselves out, and put themselves back, and then come back to the table and have to pick up the sugar lumps with their fingers.'

After the dinner-party was over and the guests had all gone home, the lady of the house said, 'Mary, I thought I told you not to forget the sugar tongs.'

'I didn't forget,' said the maid. 'I put them out as you said.'

'Well I didn't see them on the table,' said the mistress of the house.

'I didn't put them on the table,' said Mary. 'I put them in the toilet.'

A self-made industrialist was very proud of his beautiful young daughter and lavished every luxury on her. He sent her to a good school and then to college; and finally, as he was anxious for her to learn all the social graces, he sent her to an expensive finishing school in Switzerland where he hoped she would learn how to be a proper lady.

When she came home at the end of her education, he found her one morning with tears in her eyes, looking very miserable.

'What's the matter, baby?' he asked solicitously.

'Oh, Dad,' she said, 'when I was over in Switzerland, I met this very handsome and charming ski instructor. We only went out once, but, Dad . . . I'm . . . I'm pregnant!'

'You're what!' he stormed. 'What was the name of this rotten swine?'

'I don't know,' she sobbed. 'I didn't get his name.'

'You didn't get his name!' shrieked her father. 'I spend £25,000 to give you lessons in etiquette and you didn't have the courtesy to ask, "With whom am I having the pleasure?"'

A fellow went on holiday to a small town in Wales. It was a very quiet place and one evening he asked the hotel barman if it was possible to get a woman for the night.

'Nothing like that here,' said the barman. 'You want to go out and find yourself a nice sheep.'

The guest did so and spent the night in jail! Returning to the hotel the next day, he said to the barman, 'Fine piece of advice that was – telling me to go out and get myself a nice sheep!'

'Well,' said the barman, 'you didn't have to pick the police sergeant's own sheep!'

The young bride-to-be was rather ignorant of the facts of life, so she asked her mother to enlighten her.

'Well, dear,' said her mother, somewhat embarrassed, 'on the first night of the honeymoon, he'll take you up to the bedroom and undress you, and then he'll put you on the bed and take all his clothes off, and then . . . then . . . well, then he'll scare you!'

On the first night of the honeymoon, everything went as the mother had predicted. Shortly after the first time the marriage had been consummated, the young bride said, 'Darling – scare me again!' The groom duly obliged. But this happened another four times in the space of an hour!

When the bride said for the seventh time, 'Scare me again, darling!' the exhausted groom opened his weary eyes and said, 'Boo!'

A lady took her little chihuahua to the vet and said that the little dog was off his food and generally run-down.

'He's got too much hair,' said the vet. 'You want to buy some depilatory cream and get some of that excess hair off him, then he'll be as right as rain.' So she went to the chemist and asked for a tube of hair-removing cream.

The chemist said, 'There you are, madam, this should do the trick. Just rub it into your legs once a night before going to bed.'

'Oh, it isn't for my legs,' she said. 'It's for my little chihuahua.'

'In that case,' said the chemist, 'you should use it sparingly – and don't ride your bike for a couple of weeks.'

A *Final Selection of Rugby Club Riddles*

Why are people who practise coitus interruptus like British Rail trains?
They never pull out on time.

Why did God create man?
Because you can't teach a vibrator to mow the lawn.

BALDI

What happens when you cross an elephant with a prostitute?

A hooker who does it for peanuts and never forgets you.